Soaring
Along with
God's
Love

Lottie Lindsey

Trilogy Christian Publishers
A Wholly Owned Subsidiary of Trinity Broadcasting Network
2442 Michelle Drive | Tustin, CA 92780
Copyright © 2025 by Lottie Lindsey

All Scripture quotations, unless otherwise noted, taken from THE HOLY BIBLE, NEW INTERNATIONAL VERSION®, NIV® Copyright © 1973, 1978, 1984, 2011 by Biblica, Inc.® Used by permission. All rights reserved worldwide.

Scripture quotations marked (KJV) taken from *The Holy Bible, King James Version*. Cambridge Edition: 1769.

All rights reserved, including the right to reproduce this book or portions thereof in any form whatsoever.

For information, address Trilogy Christian Publishing

Rights Department, 2442 Michelle Drive, Tustin, CA 92780.

Trilogy Christian Publishing/ TBN and colophon are trademarks of Trinity Broadcasting Network.

For information about special discounts for bulk purchases, please contact Trilogy Christian Publishing.

Trilogy Disclaimer: The views and content expressed in this book are those of the author and may not necessarily reflect the views and doctrine of Trilogy Christian Publishing or the Trinity Broadcasting Network.

10 9 8 7 6 5 4 3 2 1

Library of Congress Cataloging-in-Publication Data is available.

ISBN 979-8-89597-238-0 | ISBN 979-8-89597-239-7 (ebook)

"'Though you soar like an eagle and make your nest among the stars, from there I will bring you down,' declares the Lord" (Obadiah 1:4 NIV).

ACKNOWLEDGMENTS

I want to thank those that have made this book possible. First and foremost, our Heavenly Father, for giving me the strength to believe in myself, to step out of my comfort zone. He has given me wisdom to study the Word more by writing this book.

I also want to thank Shadow and Jackie's fan page for allowing me to use some of their photos and information they teach on eagles.

I also want to thank my husband for spending the money on my camera and lens and for driving me at times when he's available on our eagle search trips.

My aunt Donna, my daughter Jonnah, and my husband, thank you for helping me come up with a title. My best birding buddies Linda Hine and Steve Wunderle, thank you for taking me and teaching me the basic ins and outs of wildlife photography.

Preface

I am a Christian, wife, mother, and grandmother. I love the Lord and am trying to find pure joy in what He gives me to see in my world. I am a retired Cosmetologist, and that retirement was taken place due to health issues. I had previously worked at the VA Medical Center for thirteen years as a patient support assistant.

One year after a major stress in my life, I came down with fibromyalgia. The doctor said it had a lot to do with trauma or auto immune disease. I knew my pain was real all over, and I didn't want to get out of bed. I had absolutely no self-worth; I felt I was a failure in every aspect of my life. Stress was taking its toll on me.

Life has always been a struggle for me, even when I truly thought I was living for Christ. Not that I don't think I was saved, though still in a rut and deep sadness, due to not knowing the power the Lord gives us to tell Satan to get behind me. It seemed that one thing would pass and another surface. I dealt with all of that by working and staying busy to keep my mind off the things tearing me apart. With my mind on business of life and keeping occupied, I didn't have to deal with what was beneath the surface.

I knew my life was so blessed, but at the same time,

Soaring Along with God's Love

my heart was just so burdened. Enjoying life was in small spurts, not a daily basis. I used to enjoy my activities after work, my house, cooking, baking, sewing, embroidery, family, riding my horse, small goat farm, and loving on my beagle.

My husband worked pretty much daylight to dark most days as a highway maintainer and self-employed cattle farmer.

Now things are changing as I see all of that will pass away, but the love for me from Jesus never will. He loves us unconditionally, and that I had never allowed to sink in. How others spoke, treated, and belittled me put a huge toll on my heart. As you read this book, I hope to show you that these are lies from Satan and how not to accept them.

I wrote this book to bring joy to others and myself, to focus on the wonderful, beautiful world our God set up for us. I took my love for the Lord Jesus and eagles to show that even in eagles you can see God and bring joy to an unusual day.

I started writing this book in January 2023 but was interrupted by other priorities. I did not have the time or the ability to focus. While at church one Sunday in 2024, our pastor mentioned that if God had given you something He wanted you to do, you should do it; you

Preface

would miss a blessing if not. So I immediately contacted Trilogy Christian Publishers to see if we could pick back up where we left off. Thankfully, I was able to move forward and resume the book.

I wrote the book mostly in my home and camper where it was quiet. While taking some free time to work on it and visiting family, I get covid again! I suddenly was quarantined. I began trying a bit more to try to complete it as soon as possible. I rebuked this round of covid and refused to accept it. All the other times, I had high fevers and was sick for weeks. I give God all the credit for no fever, rarely a cough, and fast recovery. These covid symptoms were not as bad as the other times, so little at a time, I was working to finish this book. Right after covid, I came down with E-coli and UTI; Satan sure didn't want this book finished. He may as well give up because I'm not going to give in or give up. If this book helps one person, I have accomplished what I felt God wanted me to do.

Table of Contents

Acknowledgments. 5

Preface. 7

Why An Eagle. 13

Introduction. 15

Chapter One: My Background 21

    The Personal Change 34

Chapter Two: Birding Fun 43

    Journaling. 46

    All The Ways (Song) 48

Chapter Three: Facts About Eagles. 51

Chapter Four: Principles To Follow 57

    Think Before You Act. 59

Chapter Five: The Refuge. 63

Chapter Six: Eagle Watching In Alton, Il 69

Chapter Seven: A Great Deal Of Thought 77

Chapter Eight: Jackie And Shadow. 83

    About The Group Fobbv 83

    Jackie And Shadow 85

    Discovery. 86

    Live Streaming. 86

    Dynamics 87

    Habitat 87

    Internet Fame. 87

    Pure Joy 88

    Nest Renovations. 89

    Dinner Time 89

Soaring Along with God's Love

Fiona And Fast Freddie 90

History Of Chicks 90

Nesting Time 91

Chapter Nine: Why Do I See The Holy Spirit 101

Chapter Ten: Prison Fellowship 105

Chapter Eleven: Scriptures To Build On. 113

Self-Worth 113

Anxiety/Worry 114

Entering Into Victory 116

Final Closing Thoughts. 119

Notes: Permissions 125

Why an Eagle

So much of my joy came from photographing eagles and watching their actions. One day, the Lord gave me a word that I might reach other people with my love from God through my love for the eagles. And here we are. I hope this book will bring you joy, and you can see even in the midst of pain and many other things in life that bring you down that there is always something God had in store for you to enjoy.

I hope you can learn from my experience as you read this book about not allowing yourself to be consumed with brokenness and feelings of hopelessness. This book describes how the love of wildlife (created by God) can bring strength and hope to a lot of negative thoughts. Thoughts that come in someone's heart and mind by the evil one, Satan. Falling in love with Jesus transforms many things about life, such as being able to see through clear eyes for the things about life and finding joy in it. Learning how to love yourself is a must! You will not learn to love anyone else to the fullest without loving yourself. My main purpose is to keep my joy in Christ and be a light to shine for Him, and others want what I have.

I have learned so much the last few years. I still have

Soaring Along with God's Love

my days that joy is hard to find, but if I could focus daily like I speak about, life would be much fuller. Getting into the Word of God is the best thing I can do. Praying before I vent to a friend is also helpful (I wish that was my action plan daily, but we are not perfect and fail time to time). Like I say, I still have a long way to go, even though I am getting the picture. Sometimes, life gets us down, but that is against what Jesus teaches us about how to deal with life in healthy ways. Health issues are a bondage that stops you from celebrating your blessing if you are not careful.

"Rejoice in the Lord always, I will say it again: Rejoice! Let your gentleness be evident to all. The Lord is near. Do not be anxious about anything, but in every situation by prayer and petition, with thanksgiving, present your requests to God. And the peace of God, which transcends all understanding will guard your hearts and your minds in Christ Jesus" (Philippians 4:4-7, NIV).

Introduction

I want to share with you in hopes that you can improve in your life what things are to matter the most: putting God first! Sometimes life can get us down, and I know it sure does me. Even in those time of pain and sorrow, I do my best to be thankful for what I have. Jesus didn't like strife or complaining, but it's something us humans have to learn the hard way. I try to keep myself distant from those that hurt or put me down.

You can always tell those that want to help you; they pull you out of the dark place and put hope in your heart. They stand up for you behind your back and have unconditional love. Protect your heart and mind just as the eagle protects its surroundings, mate, nest, eggs, or eaglets.

You will be reading a lot on scripture, positive changes, healthy boundaries, and the way gorgeous eagles can bring hope and enjoyment. I want you to see how God is hearing your prayers and is never going to leave you. I will be speaking of my own failures as well as incidents that broke my heart and made it hard and bitter.

I remember singing (Just As I Am) at a little old

Soaring Along with God's Love

country church I attended as a child. It was the sweetest place, and I wanted to be there as much as I could. Even at thirteen I could feel God's presence when I accepted Jesus in my heart. I would have loved a good foundation that would have kept me in that life spot. Life is life, and things change us, and choices form us to what tomorrow may bring. If you were brought up with the foundation of the love of God, remember to thank Him for that blessing. When you don't know or understand, that is ignorance and not your fault. As we are adults, we should try to educate ourselves through worshiping Jesus and studying His Word.

I will be mentioning many examples of overcoming pain and enjoying the beautiful sights God gave us when he created this world on earth for us but, most of all, the change God has made in me, even when I thought everyone else needed to change. That was not painless or easy, either; I wish I had known what I do now, and I feel so excited to know there is so much more about life that I have never experienced through the life of Jesus Christ. I was told that I should put Jesus first, then my spouse, then children, and then the church. Things fall into place easier and with better turnout, especially for my witnessing for the Lord. If we put Jesus first, that is the best way because He will direct us in the other things

Introduction

following. As I mentioned earlier: Protect your heart from negativity in all ways. That's impossible for some, and it was extremely hard for me. Most of us do have times of sadness and doubt. We just have to stay in the Word of God to overcome it and be productive for God's kingdom. Praise Him in the storms of life.

I hope to share a lot of traits the eagles have in comparison to the teachings of Jesus. God blesses us so much in so many ways; we need to have our heart and mind in the right place, being thankful for everything we enjoy, even if it is a critter. I never thought of things like this until I got interested in watching the wildlife. I felt the excitement even more every time I saw an eagle. I do hope after reading this book you feel the excitement as I do. I have people riding with me, waiting to see why I get so excited; shortly after, I will receive a photo from friends saying they saw an eagle and thought of me. I want you to think of our Creator and know He loves you.

I am constantly watching poles, trees, bodies of water, and anywhere I think an eagle may be. They are my favorite wildlife birds to watch, and it totally changes my mood, and I'm filled with blessings each time I spot one. I do want to add that our joy in the Lord comes from Him, not an eagle. At the same time, those birds sure have made a change in my life; they could not have done

Soaring Along with God's Love

that if there weren't a change in my heart through Christ first. That's why I think God wants me to share it.

Eagle watching is so relaxing and majestic in ways I cannot describe, to my fullest joy. I enjoy thoroughly the intense excitement each time I see one, even if it is the same bird I had seen before. I almost feel like they know how special they are and that they deserve respect, just by their facial expressions and body language. I love hearing them sing to each other on a branch of a tree.

Having a passion in life is always a positive, healthy reaction to feelings. I never thought that a bird of prey would touch my heart and give me so much joy. I am so thankful each and every time I see an eagle and get to snap a photograph. We should not go on feelings in our life, since every day can be challenging in these times. Focusing on the Lord will increase your faith and wisdom. Seeing something that brings me joy is icing on the cake. Eagles usually appear when my heart needs the reminder that God is hearing my heart. After all, He created these amazing, beautiful, smart, lovely, and fierce eagles.

God wants us to trust Him and rely on Him and not to think it's in just the ways He blessed us. Our joy in the Lord should never come from our conditions at the moment or be moved by emotion. Renewing our minds is

Introduction

what makes the whole process so much better with life. Get rid of the negative and think more positive thoughts. As you do, you will see some things I have stated in this book will be repeated. That's how I learned some of this process. When you fail, get back up and don't stay in your self-pity or regret. That sure was the hardest for me; the rut seemed to deepen each time I fell into it.

CHAPTER ONE

My Background

This part of the book is the hardest for me to write. It's not a pretty picture, although it may show you a bit of what life can do to someone and what forms them into who they are. The saying "hurt people hurt people" is so true. I have been hurt to the core, and I have hurt others too. There are many people in this world that have been through rougher times than I have.

After much prayer time, I felt if I could explain a few things without great details, hopefully it would be enough to help someone to believe in themselves, but most of all, know that GOD LOVES YOU.

I was born to my biological mother and father; my father walked out when I was six months old. Of course, I do not remember this and have only known what I have been told. I grew up knowing there was so much anger with my mother for what my birth-father did, and that is understandable. She worked two jobs so hard and was in a weak condition from not eating or resting enough.

When I was an approximately eighteen months old, she married the light of our lives. My step-dad never

Soaring Along with God's Love

made a difference in me that I was not his own. During all the chaos of life, Dad did his best. What a loving man, kind, gentle, just the best I could have asked for. I have told my mother, I know she had such hard times, but when God sent this wonderful husband and father into our lives, it was definitely a God send.

At eight years old, my little sister came along. We were a complete family, other than I wondered why my last name was not the same. Dad didn't like that, so he began the adoption process to change my name and father's name on my birth certificate. Since the absence of my biological father, I had so many unknown questions and hurts. What was so bad about me that someone could walk off, start a new family, and never reach out to me year after year? He was contacted and offered to give me up if he could pay for the adoption, since he had never given any input in my life whatsoever. He agreed after speaking with me (a nine-year-old girl), confirming this was what I wanted. I agreed this was what I wanted; he agreed and paid the cost of the adoption. My name was changed, and things seemed more normal.

I love my sister; she is a wonderful, Godly woman. Many times in my life, I wished I was more like her, and I felt I would have been loved and appreciated more. She made good choices throughout her life and married one

My Background

man, and he is an amazing husband and father just like ours was.

We were brought up in an extended family that would go years not speaking to sisters with a grandfather that was abusive, and a grandmother that was the Godliest woman I ever knew. If my grandma knew how her family fought and rejected one another after she left this world, she would have been so disappointed. That teaching never came from her; she taught us all to be as kind as we could. Funny thing is, I never saw much of the dysfunction other than my grandfather until after she passed at the age of fifty-nine.

Two months before my sixteenth birthday, I was married. Not because I was pregnant, not even because I was sexually active. My parents went on vacation with a friend of my mom's. My friend and her brother and I hung out; we talked had a good time. I walked into this after only dating my husband for a couple weeks. I was still a child and had no idea what choice I was making. My parents drove us to St. Louis, Missouri, since in Illinois you could not be married even if you had your parents' signature. It was not our idea to do this, but we agreed after it was presented. I had to drop out of high school, not on my own choice. Playing house was all over, reality set in, and I was scared and felt so alone.

Soaring Along with God's Love

On my sixteenth birthday, I wanted to erase the last two months, but that was not an option for me. So life went on as it was, and I had to learn and do the best I could.

My mother-in-law at the time taught me to cook, raise a garden, can, and sew. She was as good as a mother to me, took me to church with her, and taught me so much about unconditional love. We may not have always agreed on everything and still don't. We agree to disagree when that happens and so on. We are still close to this day, and she always encourages me in everything I do.

One year and eleven months later, I became a mom to a beautiful little girl. The struggles of being a teen mom, married, and with little help was about to consume me. We weren't in a good place for either of us. We had our good times and bad times. Money was not easy to come by, and I will leave it at that. We did love each other, and we did the best we both knew how at the time as young teens. A lot of dysfunction and sadness were present but also some really good times too. Those times were not long-lived.

I gave up fewer than two years after she was born, divorced for three weeks, and then came back again. Late January, we remarried, and a son was born in late October. Times were so hard; I would love to go into detail, because I know it could help someone else maybe

My Background

think of their decisions, but as of now, I can't do that. I did my best raising my kids at the time. I sure would do things differently if I had the chance. Choices are just that. Keep going; you can't go back. Think out what your choices could do to others in your life in the future, not just your own life. Learn from your mistakes and make the best out of it.

Twelve years after I dropped out of high school, I wanted to prove I could do something with myself. I bought a GED book and didn't take the course but studied for two months. I took the test and passed. I was so proud of myself probably for the first time. I then signed up for cosmetology courses. I finished that and passed as well. I have to give my husband at the time great credit for my accomplishments through all the bad times, because he made time to quiz me each night on my classes. I could not have done it without him.

He had hurt his back at work and received a small settlement. I had my eye on an old shack in the country. It had no roof, broken windows, and many other repairs that needed done. He took his whole settlement, bought the house, an old truck, and a water tank for our cistern (that's a well with a bottom in it to hold water for the home). One year later, we moved into that old house. Friends and family helped us do the work, and it was so

Soaring Along with God's Love

pretty on the inside. The outside was one of those old homes with two front doors on the porch.

It was late fall, and I got on a ladder with coat and gloves at forty-five degrees and painted that old house as far up as I could reach. I still have neighbors from that area mention they couldn't believe the determination we had for a home of our own. It was paid for, and it was home. A lot of drinking went on while everyone was helping, and no matter what I did, I couldn't get it stopped. That was the straw that broke the camel's back with all the other things that went on at that time.

We were married fifteen years, and I left after a huge fight. I thought life was rough then, but it only kept getting worse. I just could not get over the depression and hopelessness. Over half my life was married and working hard. This was a huge shock to my heart and system. My daughter staying with me and my son staying with his dad in the end was a terrible decision that could not be corrected in court. That's another story I have to stay away from for now. I carried the guilt for agreeing to that decision for over thirty years.

I thought I could not be happy without someone to love me. The good parts of my first marriage I thought would always be there with anyone else. I thought things had to get better; someone would appreciate me and

My Background

make me feel loved. I just wanted a normal, happy, loving home. We were a dysfunctional family a lot of the time. Evidently, I wasn't learning from my mistakes and was still looking for a man to make me happy and not what God had in store for me.

So only two weeks after the divorce, I met someone else and we were married six months later. That didn't turn out so well either. I didn't know how to be single since half of my life already was a married young person. The second marriage only lasted ten months after I found out my husband married me because he felt sorry for me and he thought I was pretty. I then felt I was useless and everything was my fault. Super depression, crying because I could not fix anything that had went wrong—I thought that I was sad before, and this just intensified.

Later that year after the divorce, I met someone else. Two and a half years later, we were married. I was sure that this one would be a perfect life since I waited and we got to know each other. There was so much turmoil with his family right out the gate, and I knew then I had made another huge mistake. I hung in there, refusing to go through another divorce. Any plans we made were never completed. Our home plans, building: I pretty much felt as if I lived in a compound doing what others expected of me. I went to a wedding of his family member, and

Soaring Along with God's Love

he asked for me to be in the picture. One family member said she disapproved, and I was totally devastated. Another family member told me I was not supposed to marry him because I had two kids, even though another family member married someone with two kids and nothing was said to them. I mentioned that and was informed that those kids don't come around. Wow, I couldn't believe what I just heard. My husband didn't have children. He treated mine as his own; actually, I think he would have been harder on his own children. My daughter still calls him Dad from the beginning. She has the love she always wanted and respect from him. My son resented him from day one, but at this time, I think he has realized just how good a man his step-dad is.

I remember a man in town many times would tease me and say, "It must be nice to be married to a wealthy man and drive a new car." At the time, I was taking care of myself. I paid my own car payment and my own bills. I still lived strapped, and my husband lived as he always had. I'm not saying he never helped me or gave me anything, but it wasn't as people thought. It wasn't a marriage at all. I wasn't raised that way, and my first marriage, as bad at times as it could be, was not that way either.

I loved him so much I thought things would work

My Background

out. No one knows what goes on behind closed doors or in nice a family that wants control.

My husband knows what I am writing, and he agreed I could put anything I felt. He knows now the pain it caused our marriage and the bitterness that grew in my heart for our entire situation. It was wrong of both of us to allow such behavior to steel our joy for one another and lose what we had for each other. We both still loved each other, but everytime I was given no choice to our decisions I was outraged and lost respect for him and his family. I knew I wasn't wanted and only tolerated.

We had an ice storm the winter before my mother-in-law passed away. No power, nothing but two kerosene heaters to heat and cook with. It was Valentine's Day, and I prepared a T-bone steak meal with fried potatoes and baked beans all on top of those heaters. We ate by candlelight that night, and I could feel the love in our home. I asked her if she ever thought she would spend Valentine's Day with a dinner in these situations. I think that very time of the storm created healing and love for both of us. She was the sweetest woman and would never have been so distant if others in the family weren't feeding her negativity. After ten days staying with us, life was so fulfilling. She would ask John how Tiny my beagle was and how I was. She was sick one day and

Soaring Along with God's Love

had been feeling ill for some time. I went down the lane to where she lived to check on her. She was so ill, I called my husband to come home and call an ambulance. This was in May that year. I can still see her wave at me as they took her on that gurney out the door. We all took turns staying with her. She had a colonoscopy and something went wrong. They found cancer in her colon, which explains all the pain and discomfort she had been experiencing. I remember telling her she had to get well so we could get back in our gardens. She shook her head no, and it broke our hearts. She loved her grand kids and kids. She had always been told what to do, and she had no way of knowing how to fix it. But Jesus fixed it just a few months earlier. John and I have memories of us hearing her pray at night, knowing that was an amazing blessing. Oh, how we miss her!

It's like one bad apple spoils the others in the bag if not taken care of. Pushing things under the rug so to speak didn't help a thing. Today, my husband and I have been married twenty-seven years. We are very happy and enjoy being together. We do our best to talk out things and agree to disagree when possible. We have both made mistakes through these twenty-seven years, and most of them were from no communication or respect. We still hit hard times, speak before we think now and then, but life

My Background

is so much fuller.

My husband accepted Christ in 2015, and slowly things began to change. His eyes were opened to how God expects a man to love his wife. It took many years even after that, but today I can say we will serve God in our home together and give God credit for our blessed life. I wouldn't want to do life without him.

I can remember when we decided to marry; I spoke to a pastor at a church I attended at that time. I told him I was concerned about the scripture that we are not to be unequally yoked. The pastor was a great man, and I looked up to him. He said, "You are right; that scripture is true, but he is a good man, and think how great it will be when he is saved." All I want to say about this is, you know what you read in your Bible; make sure that is your source of Godly advice, not a person's opinion. If I had waited till we were equally yoked, it may have made a huge difference in our marriage for decades of pain.

My son is a forty-two-year-old man now and has been an addict twenty-five years that I know of. That story will be in another chapter. I was at blame for leaving his dad, and all that was on my shoulders, not considering what was coming from both sides. My son has had jail sentences, prison sentences, many rehabs, ups, and downs. I have given his future and his life to the Lord, and I have tried my hardest to change things, and no one will change until they decide to. I have peace now about this, and I am not accepting the blame for it anymore. I have asked God to heal his addiction and to take care of him. As a mother of an addict, it is the worst thing I have ever lived through for as many years as this has been. I give God the glory; as of now, my son is clean and working a job.

My daughter, now forty-four, had her hard times as well, following my footsteps in broken relationships. But she rebound and is married and has a seventeen-year-old son, who is my pride and joy. My daughter chose to not be defeated, she fought for her education and leads a successful life. She has a husband that loves her, and they also have conquered their challenges. In saying these things about my children, I want to add that any choice we make in life isn't for only the time being. It affects those in your life now and forever. None of my life experiences are to blame, but myself. I allowed myself to be manipulated, hurt, and get bitter. How we live is trickled down to our own children. Dysfunction is passed down because that is what they are taught. As I look back, it's like a lukewarm life. Going to church but living a life that is not pleasing to God is not a good example.

When I mentioned to my daughter I was going to be

My Background

writing this book and putting things in there that hurt and that were touching some personal things, she agreed it was fine. She also said to me that the reason she had bad relationships is because she thought it was okay to settle, because I had. Then she chuckled and said, put in your book, "I know I am good person; I just picked the wrong people."

The only thing that kept me sane was the love of the Lord. I didn't know much, but I knew I was saved, and God loved me. But in all that, the depression and mental torment got worse by the year.

Just before covid came along, I was down to 100 lbs. I remember being in a group place, sitting alone, and a lady walked past me and said, "Can't you smile?" That broke my heart, since I had supported her when she had cancer; she cried a lot, and I never said anything like that to her. It was a horrible nightmare with my physical and emotional well-being. I had fibromyalgia, was diagnosed with back and neck issues, and now have MGUS (Monoclonal gammopathy of undetermined significance, a condition where the body produces an abnormal protein called an M-Protein). My Hematologist has to check every six months for progression. I could or could not go into Multiple Myeloma, a form of blood cancer that destroys bone. I always accepted what a doctor would

Soaring Along with God's Love

tell me, until I knew God wants us well. So I keep the hope that progression may never come to me. Once we got the diagnosis and dealt with it and the weight came back on, I realized the stress was probably what caused the weight loss to that extent. That is just my perspective. So far, my MGUS disease hasn't progressed any; I'm still stable. It may or may not ever progress, and I am relying on the Lord for a positive report. I have many health issues along with this, and it changed my life drastically. I'm learning more scripture and rebuking Satan even in sickness. At the same time, I'm trying to learn to get away from the things that stress me out and lean towards things opposite, just like eagles.

The Personal Change

While COVID mandates were going strong and the feeling of seclusion as well as fear of what was to come was overwhelming, my depression seemed to skyrocket. My daughter insisted I speak with a counselor, which I did. I found a Christian one and still speak with her to this day. I don't have to very often, but sometimes I need a bit of an adjustment to my thoughts. I always thought it was silly and wouldn't change a thing. I learned that knowing how much Jesus loved me and how to love myself made a

My Background

huge difference.

I began to slowly change, by watching teaching on Christian TV programs, reading many positive books of Christian growth, and studying God's Word. The more I worshiped Jesus, the better I felt. I fed myself on Christian music instead of depressing songs that bring in the negative memories or sadness. As knowledge began seeping into my mind and heart, I just wanted more of the Word of God. I didn't want to be out of the habit of church, so I got more than I was used to, via the internet, books, music, and TV programs.

Before this change from my self-confidence, life just didn't seem so happy or worth waking up each day. A lot of crying, doubt, hopelessness, and a huge spirit of negativity just consumed me. Life can make you better or bitter, and at that time, mine was going more toward the bitter side.

Years after my counseling had started and healing began to renew my mind, I could see a difference. My daughter told me one day that life choices are passed down, just like in her situation. She said to me one day something like...concerning multiple marriages and she always being on the right path of being awesome, but she picked the wrong people in seeking worthiness in relationships. Now I love myself and don't take pain and

Soaring Along with God's Love

suffering from anyone. It made me laugh that she has come so far on standing her ground. Not that we always agree, but we can have a relationship that we can talk and move on from what my past drained down to hers. Like I said: Be careful of your choices; you are not only changing your life but those that come after you.

As you read this book, I hope you see how you can make a stagnant life bloom and become a thriving and hopeful one full of joy of the Lord. Does life produce joy daily? NO! I get more joy from life, my hobby, and more things than I used to. It took a lot of work, setting boundaries for myself and others, changing habits, and refocusing, and I am still trying to renew my mind the way Jesus wants us to. I have to have peace, or I am an emotional mess. I have tried to stay away from those that discourage me or belittle me. It is not that I am doing away with them; it's that I am taking care of my mental health. I don't need to be in a spotlight, but I sure don't want to be put down. As followers of Christ, we should build each other up and encourage one another. I try to stay away from discussions that pull me back into a pit of despair and depression. Guarding our hearts and minds is a must.

"Therefore encourage one another and build each other up, just as in face you are doing" (1 Thessalonians

My Background

5:11, NIV).

We want people to love and respect us; we are allowed to control what we accept and refuse to gravitate to. I learned that from my daughter as she was trying to help me not be so negative and sad. She builds me up and encourages me to be myself. She has said many times, "Be happy, Mom, do the things you like to do. Do not let others set your standard mood for the day." Then she taught me about manipulation. It only made me feel guilty and would exhaust me. What everyone thought of me was my opinion of myself. That was so wrong, and I had to decide to believe what Jesus thought of me and not what others said about me or how they treated me.

I mainly depend on Jesus to guide and change me inside and out. Don't fool yourself: That does not happen overnight. Life is still life, and I still fail, get sad, grumpy, lose my patience, and lose my joy in difficult times. I do know that my joy in the Lord should never change. He doesn't change, so why should we allow our thoughts of what He thinks of us change?

I usually know what brings me joy, and that's where the eagles come in. First and foremost, I have learned you have to learn to love yourself and others, forgive yourself and others, give it to God, and leave it with Him. I don't feel that forgiving someone means allowing

Soaring Along with God's Love

them to put you down. I'm also learning that just because someone is making life hard for you, sometimes I truly believe Satan works through that. A lot of people are not happy if you don't respond the way they want you to or act as they think you should. It is taking me a long time, but I'm trying my best to let that thought pattern go by the wayside. Learn the difference from Satan's voice tormenting you to God's direction and correction, not condemnation. Life with the hope and faith in Jesus Christ can truly move a mountain of grief and unhappiness when we focus on Him first.

"How beautiful on the mountains are the feet of those who bring good news, who proclaim peace, who bring good tidings, who proclaim salvation, who say to Zion 'Your God reigns!" (Isaiah 52:7, NIV).

I am not saying life is perfect, because it never will be for Christians or non-Christians. I struggle still, and I will, but now I know who is capable of dragging me out of that pit and back into the light. Jesus is! Do you know Jesus truly loves you? He knows your faults, and he wants to help you succeed and be who you were meant to be.

"That you may be the sons of your Father in heaven: He causes his sun to rise on the evil and the good, and sends rain on the righteous and unrighteous" (Matthew 5:45, NIV).

My Background

There will always be a dart Satan will throw our way to dismantle what we have worked so hard to overcome. I used to wonder why non-Christians had an easier life than me. Someone once told me that Satan goes after what is a threat to him. He wants to take as many with him as he can. That is why you see a lot of Christians struggle, not understanding. Mostly, we don't get it because we don't read the Word and learn knowledge and wisdom.

Being a Christian sure makes it a lot easier to deal with and to be positive as much as possible and more productive in times of troubles. The Bible says many things that give us wisdom and growth. The more you read, the more you want to read. Whatever you feed your mind on is what fruit you produce. What do you feed your mind?

Dr David Jeremiah speaks of this poem that is so true:

Two natures Beat within my breast.
The one is foul...the one is blessed.
The one I hate, the one I love.
The one I feed will Dominate"

Think about this as you read it again slowly. As we sit and think negative more than positive, the negative is going to win over the positive thoughts.

Soaring Along with God's Love

God's Word says in Philippians 4:8 (NIV):

"Finally, brothers and sisters, whatever is true, whatever is noble, whatever is right, whatever is pure, whatsoever is lovely, whatever is admirable—if anything is excellent or praiseworthy— think about such things."

"I can do all everything through him who gives me strength" (Philippians 4:13, NIV).

These verses and the poem are my favorite encouragement when times get rough. Lastly, I do want you to realize that, when you want everyone around you to change, chances are you need to concentrate on what God wants to change in you. That's a tough lesson and doesn't feel so good at first. After you make a change, you won't find so much fault with others. Your heart changes, and God works with your heart and mind to renew your thinking and give you the best hope and love you will ever know.

"Do not conform any longer to the pattern of this world, but be transformed by the renewing of your mind. Then you will be able to test and approve what God's will is his good, pleasing and perfect will" (Romans12:2, NIV).

Be the best you can be; do the best you can do. When you fail, get back up, ask God to give you wisdom on how to handle things of this sort again His way. Should

My Background

it come that you owe an apology, give it, and if it's not accepted, that is not on you. A Christian should always accept an apology from another follower. Forgiveness is given; trust is earned.

CHAPTER TWO

Let's Get to the Happy Times

Birding Fun

Linda and I made many trips to the river levees, refuge, Alton, IL, and just plain birding trips to see what we could photograph. She took a lot of time with me to teach me to set my camera on manual. I always thought I would never get a good photo, although Linda would say, "Oh, yes you will." She is such an encouraging person and mentor for me in this time of learning.

We went to photograph a snowy owl (I had never seen one before), many other owls, birds, and eagles as well as their nests.

There were many times we would just go for a drive. Linda and her elderly friend, Steve, were very close, and she introduced me to him. I can remember Steve so worried about me when I was so thin and sick. He taught me so much about the camera as well. I would be out and about at the refuge looking for birds to take photos of. I would see his truck and stop and chat a bit. We would end up talking for an hour about our cameras and birds. He was the dad connection I didn't have anymore. He would be so patient to sit and explain things many times to me about different settings and the birds. He was so smart about the birds and loved teaching me all about them. He and Linda would get me out in the refuge, and we would sit in chairs till I saw something new and got a photo. I never would have learned this passion without the two of them. I hadn't seen patience in someone since my dad was alive.

I remember one of the last times I sat with Steve; he wanted to show me this bird that would sit on his truck mirror. I couldn't imagine his excitement as he shared it with me. Sure enough, we pulled up, and that little yellow warbler just looked in his truck window. We took so many of different views of that little bird. But both of us enjoyed the eagles. It seemed to be our first choice of bird to photo. Steve passed recently, and he is so missed. I was listening to my voice mails one day and heard his voice. It shook me to the core. What a great, loving, kind man he was. He had to be the kindest man, encouraging and smart. His wife was so kind to allow me to speak of him in this book. She knew what Steve meant to Linda and me and what we meant to him. Linda was like a family member to him herself. Linda spent so much time taking him birding. He enjoyed it so much, and it was

Let's Get to the Happy Times

a way to pay it forward for him. I wish I had been able
to spend more time the last year with him; I had other
responsibilities and was not able to. I still have his voice on
my voice mail, and I will never intentionally remove it.

Think positive instead of negative. As a younger
woman, I had in my mind that someone else would be the
one to make me happy. Such a lie to tell yourself: if only
I had just allowed Jesus to fill me where that void was,
be happy with myself, and not wait for someone else to
bring joy. I found that didn't work out.

Are you wondering where this story is headed? I'm
sure you are; let me try to clear it up for you. Life is
hard, we can either learn to find happiness and joy in
it or become consumed by pain and agony. No one is
ever going to be perfect, and don't think that is what
is expected of you. Learn to enjoy your life and make
the most of it. Mine was out of control with stress and
heartache, which turned to bitter sadness.

I have always felt like a black sheep. That's a lot
to have on your shoulders. The past year even proved
through some things that took place in my life. I felt of
no value to others and only acceptable when I was doing
for them. Giving is more important than receiving; that is
what keeps me going when I feel unappreciated or taken
advantage of. Seems like in this world it's all about what

Soaring Along with God's Love

some folks can get from you, not what they can give. My love language is service (the little things) I love to do for others.

Recently, I had an older gentlemen tell me that the eagle was a sign of strength. We will get more into the stories of the eagles as the book continues. They are magnificent, beautiful, smart, and very attentive. I'm sure you will look at my photos and see the crazy love that comes with seeing God's creation. I have owned it and loved every minute of it. Maybe that is just why I love them so much: I wish I had their strength. Of course, I do through the Lord; He never leaves us.

Journaling

One night while I was writing in my journal, I noticed the words were not usually what I would write. I kept writing on and on, until I thought that must have been from the Lord telling me something. So I wrote it on a piece of paper and kept it in my purse.

I gave it to a young man at church that wrote his own songs, and I asked him to look at it and see what he thought. That next Sunday, he asked me if he could sing it. I was shocked that it worked out to be a song. He was a friend of mine's son that I loved dearly. A couple years

Let's Get to the Happy Times

after that, he left the church, and shortly after, so did I. I wrote him, asking for the music he used, but he never responded.

Now I'm in a different church that teaches me deeper than I ever thought I would go. It is a small church, and that doesn't bother me because I love learning, and the Bible says narrow is the way. Well narrow is in numbers as well. I have missed out on so much by not being in this church before. But I do believe God had a plan. One of the women in my church now went to college to write music. I gave her the words and asked her if she could write music for the song. She has been working on it and is almost done. I'm so excited to hear it sung at our church. I want to add it in this book so you can see how God works in mysterious ways. I hope someday I can help others by writing books and songs to encourage and bring people to Christ.

I'm going to include it, but I must tell you this is under the copyright law. Please do not use my song for anything without my permission or legal agreement.

Soaring Along with God's Love

All The Ways
written by Lottie Lindsey
Copyrighted

Hey God
It's me again
I just came to you to say
Every day I am more amazed
By your love
And faithfulness
I'm so thankful that I can
Count on you when times are bad and rough

(Pre-chorus)
My heart is hard
But my worries are
All in your hands

(Chorus)

Show me all the ways
To represent you great
Show me exactly when and where to go
Let me be a light
Shining for you so bright
Take me and use me, mold me to your own

Today
I'm not afraid
Of anything
That comes my way
Cause you have shown me all the ways

Let's Get to the Happy Times

(Verse)
Hey God
You are so good
You pick me up
When I feel like the world is caving in

(Pre-chorus)

You'll be my strength
When I am weak
I'll live by your guide

(Chorus)

Show me all the ways
To represent you great
Show me exactly when and where to go
Let me be a light
Shining for you so bright
Take me and use me, mold me to your own

Today
I am not afraid
Of anything
That comes my way
Cause you have shown me all the ways

(Bridge)

When family falls apart
You can mend every heart
When my health goes down hill
You tell me, peace be still
When relationships are strained

Soaring Along with God's Love

I'll look to you to show me all the ways
(Chorus)

Show me all the ways
To represent you great
Show me exactly when and where to go
Let me be a light
Shining for you so bright
Take me and use me, mold me to your own

Today
I'm not afraid
Of anything
That comes my way
Cause you have shown me all the ways
Show me all the ways
(repeat)
(repeat)
Oh, all the ways

CHAPTER THREE

Facts About Eagles

I am going to start with eagle facts so when I begin the stories you have a bit of background about them if you haven't been educated about them. I want to add, this is what I have learned from books I have read and the internet or friends telling me. You may find facts of different info, and I do not state that mine are exact, but I will say that it sure had increased my desire to learn more and see God in their actions. It's almost like a study guide for me. I watch these magnificent birds, and I see God's

Soaring Along with God's Love

teaching in them for me. I have the desire to learn what God wants me to learn and enjoy doing it. So between reading books and watching videos from various authors and television presentations for years, it has given me the desire to learn more. I have an imagination, and the eagles fit right in with it. So here we go with some facts about these beautiful birds and family devotions they share.

Eagles can fly up to thirty-mph and can dive at speeds up to 100 mph.

Fledgling (baby) eagles learn to fly at three months of age

Eagles can live thirty years or more in the wild.

Male bald eagles are smaller than females.

Eagles' eyesight is five times that of a human.

They can fly as high as 10,000 feet.

An eagle sneeze is called a snite.

A grown eagle has around 7,000 feathers.

The juvenile eagles are the ones after they fledged the nest and up until their head and tail feathers go the solid white. Eagles may be brown and white mixed over their bodies until they are four to six years old, when they turn dark brown and have white heads and tail feathers. You will see the eagle appearance change in the progression photo above.

Facts About Eagles

Eagles start building and renovating their nest in fall, depending where the birds are living, to build their nests or add on to the one they have used for years. While it is true that eagles build on their nest all the time, during fall their primary focus is preparing the nest specifically for egg laying, incubation, and raising their chick(s).

The big sticks being brought in provide a dual purpose; a crib barrier (quad rails for the crib, so to speak) keeps chicks safely in the nest bowl until they are old enough to begin the practice of perching and branching.

Smaller branches are used for shaping and fortifying the nest and nest bowl; often, larger sticks are broken down to be placed just right. As we all know how particular our Shadow and Jackie are, if you don't, you most likely will if you watch any videos or can see the excitement in my story.

Fluff is a soft material the eagles bring into the nest bowl, or center of the nest, to create a soft, warm nursery just right for eggs and chicks. Each territory provides a different type of available fluff. For Jackie and Shadow, it is typically consisting of pine needles, grasses, reeds from the shoreline. Normally we won't see signs of fluff until Jackie is ready to start the egg-laying process, with more

Soaring Along with God's Love

delivered often after eggs are laid.

The new season is beginning, and Jackie and Shadow leave us looking forward to what is up their birdie sleeves. Historically, egg laying season for Big Bear area is January through April every year.

Some older nests are four to six feet in diameter and three feet deep; some can even be bigger. The largest one was found in Petersburg, Florida: 9.5 feet diameter and 20 feet deep at almost 6,000 pounds. A full-size nest can weight up to 1,000 pounds. They have the largest nest of any other birds. Can you imagine a tree strong enough to hold a nest that big or heavy? Sometimes the tree can't support the heavy nest in a windstorm. They carry the sticks to the nest as needed to support their fledglings.

One full-grown eagle can weight up to seventeen pounds and stretch at least six feet across when the wings are out flying. The mates stay together for life (except for one I know, Jackie and Shadow). Shadow loved Jackie and ran off from Mr. B (her first mate) for the love of his life. Jackie and Shadow are the ones I watch and the ones I got permission to write about in this book. You will read a lot about them and the love they have for one another.

The eagles work hard to be prepared for the eggs and hatching process. They take turns going for food and sitting on the eggs, although Jackie will not allow

Facts About Eagles

Shadow to sit on her eggs when there is snow present on the nest. She doesn't move for days. He will bring her food, and she will shake off the snow and position herself right back on that nest of eggs.

Since we know eagles fly the highest, the Native Americans I have been told believe that they are the closest to the Creator. The Native Americans saw the Eagles as a symbol of strength, leadership, and vision. Eagle symbolism also includes loyalty, devotion, freedom, truth, honor, hope, foresight, and awareness. I can see where that understanding would come to mind.

The mortality rate for bald eagles is high during their first year of life, with the U.S. Fish and Wildlife Service estimating it greater than fifty percent. Rain, snow, and cold temperatures can be dangerous for chicks because they are too big to be fully covered by their mother.

The figure of the eagles' wings was also used in the Old Testament to represent the strength and loving kindness of the Lord in delivering His covenant people.

Exodus 19:4 (NIV): "You yourselves have seen what I did to the Egyptians, and how I carried you on eagles' wings and brought you to myself."

Deuteronomy 32:11 (NIV): "Like an eagle stirs up its nest, and hovers over its young, that spreads its wings to catch them and carry them aloft."

Soaring Along with God's Love

CHAPTER FOUR

Principles to Follow

I think of several leadership principles that we can learn from eagles. Stay away from narrow-minded people, those that bring you down and don't see any good in life. That is actually a negative thought that will not produce good fruit (meaning showing your life as living as a godly person). Eagles stay together as a pair that reflect love on each other.

Have a vision and remain focused no matter what the obstacles bring into your life. Just like the eagle stays focused on their hunting food, building a nest, caring for the eggs, eaglets, and each other.

You will succeed as God plans out for you when remaining positive and hopeful. These are not traits I have always shown; that is why it takes away our witness for the Lord. If we want others to see our love and hope in Christ, we must produce good, positive fruit.

Faith is the main action that will go a long way in your witness for Jesus. You don't see eagles lose. They stay focused to do what needs to be done, even if it's sitting in a nest full of snow around it for days.

Ask the Holy Spirit to direct your moods, mouth, and

Soaring Along with God's Love

actions every morning. Try to stay focused and not lose faith. If you know today is not going to be a day that is going to take place, pray about it and limit the people you share your attitude with until you have time with Jesus. The Holy Spirit will give you knowledge and faith that you can shine your light to others as a follower of Jesus. Then they will see your fruit and want what you have.

When we go around sad, angry, bitter, and moping around like the sky is falling, what are we showing others? If you believe God can do anything, be sure and let it show in your life. I am preaching to the choir here. I also need to begin each day this way myself. It takes practice and studying God's Word enough to do that. Once again, it's not an overnight process, and I'm still working on it.

Don't allow Satan to discourage you into thinking negative things and produce ugly fruit. It is not a reflection of how Jesus loves us and carries us in hard times. Have the vision and remain focused no matter what the obstacles produce. You will succeed in time and will be so glad you did. A good positive mind will also increase health and wellness in your life. Remember, the eagles run off invaders from their nest and do not allow danger near their home. We should not either; this protects our children from repeating the negativity we

Principles to Follow

produce and carry down to them. Protecting your family is the same as how an eagle protects their environment in teaching their young. Eagles soar, and so should we when we have the love of Jesus in our hearts.

Think Before You Act

I try my best to be careful what I do, to keep my witness in a good place for the Lord. None of us is perfect, and beating ourselves up for not being perfect is so wrong. I have learned that from so many people now. Not forgiving yourself is not trusting in the Lord. He says He forgave you when you asked, so believe it and go on about your life. Being a Christian is not about the works you do; it's about your relationship. When you have a relationship, you will want to do things without it being work.

This last month I had covid, and it wasn't a bad case this time. I kept rebuking it daily, and I was so thankful I was still functioning. I give God all the praises for it. Just a few days after, I started feeling terribly ill, weak, and fatigued more than usual. The doctor ran tests, and I had E-coli and UTI. I had to go to the pharmacy to get my medicine. I stood in line to get to the counter; the pharmacy tech told me I needed to come back twenty-five

Soaring Along with God's Love

minutes later. I said, "It takes me thirty to get home; I will just sit in this chair and wait." I heard my name called, and I went back to the counter. I asked the same tech if he called my name. He asked the pharmacist, and he said, "Yes, her medicines are ready." Oh, I was so glad; my legs were terribly weak. The tech didn't make eye contact with me but told me to get in line. I looked back; there were seven people in front of me, and I had never had that happen before. Usually, when they called my name, I got my medicines and went on my way. I have my credit card on file, and it takes about one minute to finalize my order. I went to the back of the line, and I told the lady in front of me that if I went down, they would have to pick me up. I was so weak, I could hardly stand. This is totally uncalled for; I was so ill and needed to sit, not stand in line for another twenty or thirty minutes. When it was my time, they had called a second tech, and I got him. It was a new medication I had never taken, so I had to go speak with the pharmacist to be sure I took it correctly. He even said he was sorry and told me to try to have a good evening.

As I left, I cried. I looked down and saw I had my favorite scripture on the shirt I was wearing: "I can do everything through Him who gives me strength" (Philippians 4:13, NIV). Did I hurt my witness again? My

Principles to Follow

husband even commented that was ridiculous of them to do that to a sick person, and he most likely would have said something too. It just kept bearing on my heart. I couldn't believe I was caught off guard again. I have made enough mistakes in my life; I do not want to be a bad witness for the Lord.

I called the pharmacy the next day and spoke to the manager in tears. I told him what happened, and I was sorry I was upset about it and commented to the lady in line about it. He said he was so sorry and glad I called and told him. He said that it was not acceptable to treat someone like he did me, and he would handle it. I told him I was a Christian and didn't want to hurt my witness to others. It didn't seem like a big deal to him, but it was to me.

As most of us, we have regrets of our pasts. We do not live there anymore, and Jesus loves us as we are. When He died on that cross, it was for us to accept his love, repent, believe, and put Him as Lord and Savior of our lives. He forgave our past, present, and future sins when we were saved.

Seems like anyone I told how upset I had reacted all said we are only human and things happen. My daughter reminded me that, if people think they have to be perfect, that is why a lot of them don't even try to go to church.

Soaring Along with God's Love

To me, it isn't about religion; it's about a relationship with the Lord. There is a difference in going to church and the mind knowledge. It's all about the heart knowledge with Jesus, winning souls for His kingdom and helping people see they are worthy and loved by Jesus. Don't forget that is the most important start for you. Know Jesus loves you and wants you happy and well. It doesn't matter what you have done that you feel you are not worthy of His love; that's Satan's lies and not true. Your sins are gone as far as the east is from the west when you repent and accept Jesus.

CHAPTER FIVE

The Refuge

    I never thought of eagles teaching me a way to serve God, until one day I drove through the refuge in our area looking to photograph a bald eagle. I was trying out my new lens I had gotten for my camera. As I was driving along slowly on the roadway, I was praying over several things in my life that I needed peace with. When life gets me down, sometimes I have to go for a ride and have a talk with Jesus, alone in a car, just us. Low and behold, guess what:

Soaring Along with God's Love

I looked to the right to see if an eagle was in the tree I had seen before. But no, it was on the ground probably ten feet from the ditch. I stopped my car, quietly opened my door, and grabbed my camera. I leaned over the hood of my SUV to be stable; many of my photos aren't clear when I can't eliminate the blur due to the shakes I have.

This bald eagle looked up at me, never acted intimidated or scared. About that time, it decided to put on a show. It jumped up and down, staring right at me! Then it picked up some dry grass and flew up and landed back down in the same place. It flapped it wings as if to say, "Hi, I see you, and we are going to have some fun." As I watched and was shooting pictures one after another, because it was not standing still, I had never before seen an eagle put on a show that close to the road and not be so sober to what was around it. I had tears in my eyes and kept shooting photos. I am sure I took over 200 pictures of it. Finally, after about twenty minutes, it decided to fly away. I was constantly shooting every move it made until it was out of sight.

I saw a car ahead of me watching the entire show. I'm sure they thought I was as funny as the eagle.

The Refuge

Soaring Along with God's Love

By this time, I was in happy tears and turned around and almost ran into a lady riding her bike through the refuge. I don't know who she was or who it scared the worst, her or me. I apologized and drove off. I called my husband with such joy, telling him about the eagle. It was as if God had allowed me to see this action to show me He hears my prayers and loves me even when I don't feel or hear Him. He knows my love for eagles and the peace they give me. I know that day was from God, and it was just the first event. My daughter even took this photo and had it canvas framed for me as a gift. It brings joy to me each time I look on the wall it hangs on.

The Refuge

We can't live on feelings alone. We must remember if anyone moves, it's not God but us. The true first love we felt when we accepted Jesus is still there; we just have to practice it. We can allow it to go stagnant, and who's fault is that? Sure isn't God's! He loves us unconditionally; when we love him back, we have His Holy Spirit directing us and guiding us if we will only follow. How is your fruit of the Spirit? Does it demonstrate a loving God, and is it showing how much respect and love you have for Him? This should all come natural for us once we learn and grow. If you never read His love letters to us and His life manual (Bible), you will never know the things that He has set before you. He is the same today as he was 2,000 years ago. People want to change His Word to match our society, and that definitely is not what I recommend. It would set your life into a tailspin that is hard to undo. His Word never changes.

Soaring Along with God's Love

    I met so many wonderful people at the refuge and got so much needed advice from others since I was just learning to take wildlife photos. The refuge was my quiet place besides my camper. The refuge has changed so much about it. We see way fewer eagles and wildlife now, but sometimes we may get lucky. They will have tours, so we can see their nest and sometimes an eagle pair in the nest. I got one shot of them mating, but that's before I had the good camera or knew really how to shoot to get a good photo.

    I enjoyed the eagle tours and the quiet time that comes with the refuge. It's God's country, and if you appreciate what He has given us, just sit still and soak it in, I'm sure you will receive a blessing.

CHAPTER SIX

Eagle Watching in Alton, Il

My friend Linda Hine and I were bird watching over a river one day in Alton, Illinois. Linda was behind me as I was taking shots at dawn on the river. The photo above is what she captured. It is a photo I will always cherish, doing what I love.

We drove to several places around Alton, over by the river, lock, and dam, and even crossed over the river on a ferry. The whole two trips we have made the last few years were nothing but amazing. I would never have gotten to do something like this if she hadn't taken me.

We were snapping photos as the action played out each place we were at. At one point, we saw three bald eagles fishing. One would swoop down and grab a fish with its talons and fly off with it, then make a circle and drop the fish. That was odd, I was thinking, because I had never seen an eagle drop a catch of anything. Just a few minutes later, there was another bald eagle fishing, and the same thing happened, and then another. I was thinking, what in the world is going on here.

As I watched the scenery, I saw there was a tree behind the water with eight juvenile eagles in it. HMMM (my imagination took over).

They are having school! I had noticed a few of the juveniles were flying, which appeared to be watching the ones fishing. Then they would return to the tree. (Usually when I have seen eagles fish, they go to a tree and perch and eat their catch; when feeding their young they take it to the nest and feed them.) I couldn't stop making up little stories to go with what we had just seen. It was the

Soaring Along with God's Love

most fun I have ever had watching such a group of eagles. Never had I seen such activities and the patience of so many eagles in one tree.

In my mind, I could see this lesson of survival and maturity being taught to these youngsters. It felt as if the tree of juveniles was a classroom, and they were all paying attention. I was thinking, so they paid attention to their parents teaching them to thrive, succeed, and have everlasting joy.

As I am thinking all of these imaginations I was making up, I also couldn't help later thinking a lot about how God teaches us. Eagles to me are amazing and just so precious. The thought that God put so much into bringing these critters to life and so beautiful. If only all humans had that desire to see others succeed and teach them.

The funny thing is I can remember in the beginning each time I would get excited, I just couldn't be quiet. My friend would say "*SHHHH.*" I think I have finally learned to keep my vocals to a whisper—well, sometimes. I would get so excited that I just couldn't contain myself.

We later watched a pair of eagles, one on the ground and one in a tree. The one on the ground caught a squirrel and took it to the tree. It did not share either! Poor thing, the one in tree just watched the other one eat it. I'm sure there was more to that story than we saw.

Eagle Watching in Alton, Il

We stayed at a lodge near the river at Alton. It was such a beautiful view. We left early and went to the river to see if there were many eagles out. There was ice on the river floating in chunks for the most part. The barges had busted it up, and it was so beautiful. I looked up above my head, and there was an eagle eating its fish breakfast on a limb.

Soaring Along with God's Love

We started walking up and down the edge of the river and saw so many bald eagles and juvenile ones floating on ice. They were so pretty and didn't want to share either. There was an abundance of fish, so none went hungry. We took so many pictures, it was overwhelming. They acted like they didn't care at all about what we were doing.

CHAPTER SEVEN

A Great Deal of Thought

I think of how large their wings are stretched out flying, and it reminds me of Jesus' arms on that cross dying for our sins so we can be in Heaven with Him someday.

"He will cover you with his feathers, and under his wings you will find refuge; his faithfulness will be your shield and rampart" (Psalm 91:4, NIV).

Seeing the eagle sitting next to his nest just watching around the tree reminds me how nice it is to sit upon a porch of our home watching the wildlife and enjoying fresh air. God wants us to appreciate the beautiful things he gave us to see and watch just like the eagles do.

Watching those juvenile eagles in that tree take in every move the older ones made teaching them to fish reminds me how God wants us to pay attention to our Christian mentors and what we learned from the Bible. The eagles have to work for what they get, and that is what God expects us to do.

"For even when we were with you, we gave you this rule: If a man will not work he shall not eat" (2 Thessalonians 3:10, NIV).

Soaring Along with God's Love

If the young eagles refused to pay attention and learn from the older ones, they would not have the ability to fish and have food to eat. The same is for us humans as we go through life. If we watch sincere followers of Christ Jesus as they live as examples to others, we will learn just how awesome learning to be Christ-like can be. We will learn to read the Word of God, love each other, and represent His love to others. Not all Christians present good qualities for us to learn from and watch. None of us is perfect, but find someone that has a good heart and loves Jesus, and see how you feel around them. If you feel the Holy Spirit from them, you know they will be an asset to your mind and soul. Whatever you hang around is what you will pick up on. Don't take any more than small doses of those that don't produce good fruit, or it will damage your witness and your attitude. It happens to me at times as well.

"Stay away from a foolish man, for you will not find knowledge on his lips" (Proverbs 14:7, NIV).

Satan knows what to use to defeat us; keeping bad company will spill over to us and deceive us.

John 10:10 (NIV) says, "Satan comes to kill, steal, and destroy. I have come that they may have life and have it to the fullest."

Life isn't about who or how you make people happy

or if they accept you. It's about pleasing God. It took a while to get that head knowledge, and sometimes it's still hard for me. Focus on the good and do your best to accept what you can't change. Satan knows exactly what he can use to disrupt your life. Usually, it is something you would never think it would be. Remember, it's always better to walk alone than to walk with a crowd going the wrong direction. If it isn't Jesus' way, stay away from it.

Matthew 7:13-14 (NIV): "Enter through the narrow gate, for wide is the gate and broad is the road that leads to destruction, and many enter through it. But small is the gate and narrow the road that leads to life, and only a few find it."

Being a worrier can take days from your life and make them very uncomfortable. It does not make anything in life any easier, just a bit frustrating.

Matthew 6:3 (NIV): "Therefore do not worry about tomorrow, for tomorrow will worry about itself. Each day has enough trouble of its own."

Luke 12:25 (NIV): "Who of you by worrying can add a single hour to his life?"

I feel unbelief is doubting the Lord; this helps me to be careful to not be negative about someone that can change. I hear people say others will never change, and that puts negative thoughts in my mind. Sometimes

Soaring Along with God's Love

people can be a roller coaster ride with drugs, addictions, or other sins. I can never give up on them, even if I know the ride is hard on me. Jesus tells us to have hope!

The Bible describes hope as a confidence in God's promises, even when they may not be immediately fulfilled.

Does it sound like Jesus wants us living the regret and fretting the way we do sometimes? God is so good. He wants us to have the joy of Christ. I'm sure it saddens Him that we choose to believe a lie Satan tells us rather than His word that He loves us and has a plan for our life.

In the time of mourning and brokenness, God pours out his love and joy for us. All we have to do is take it. I don't feel it's wrong for us to mourn or be sad, just not to the point we see no joy in the Lord. He suffered our pain and sin so that we may be forgiven if we accept Him and believe.

John 3:16 (NIV) says, "For God so loved the world that he gave his one and only Son, that whoever believes in him shall not perish but have eternal life" (Heaven rather than Hell).

Romans 15:13 (KJV) says, "May the God of hope fill you with all joy and peace as you trust in him, so that you may overflow with hope by the power of the Holy Spirit."

Romans 10:17 (KJV) says, "Consequently faith

A Great Deal of Thought

comes from hearing the message and the message is by heard through the Word of Christ."

2 Timothy 4:2 (NIV) says, "Preach the Word, be ready in season and out of season; correct, rebuke, and encourage with great patience and careful instruction" (Like the eagles and the humans teach their young).

Isaiah 40:31 (NIV) says, "But those who hope in the Lord, will renew their strength. They will soar on wings of eagles; they will run and not grow weary they will walk and not faint.

CHAPTER EIGHT

Jackie and Shadow

ABOUT THE GROUP FOBBV

I'm sharing parts of the *FOBBVCAM* that I watch to see the beauty in these two magnificent birds.

Jackie and Shadow are a pair of bald eagles that have enticed my heart to check in on these two daily. Just under normal activities they are amazing and make my heart happy. I will include part of what the group has mentioned in the beginning, and if you are interested in watching them, feel free to get a happy boost to your day. I enjoy watching them because they are one of God's creatures that brings me nothing but joy and laughter. I hope you check this out and enjoy as much as I do.

"The official *FOBBV* Big Bear Bald Eagle Group! We are an educational environmental non-profit educated to protecting and preserving the natural habitats and special species of Big Bear Valley. Our eagle nest camera was installed in 2015 under the Forest Service special use permit to observe and study the nesting behavior as well as success rates and possible issues in this mountaintop location. The nest is located in the San Bernardino Mountains at an altitude of 7,000 feet, the highest altitude bald eagle nest equipped with a camera. The cameras are streaming live 24/7/365 free of charge and free of ads.

Our Facebook group was created as a complimentary resource for the official Facebook page featuring posts and updates from *FOBBV*. A group of ten volunteers monitor and document the nest and maintain and repair the cameras. The mission of our group is to provide the opportunity for viewers to share screen captures and videos taken from our live cameras, pictures from the Big Bear area, or other creations inspired by Jackie and Shadow...Pull up a perch and share our love for Jackie and Shadow. Enjoy their antics and unique mountaintop environment. Observe, laugh, and learn with us!

Watch live on *FOBBV* YouTube channel:
https://www.youtube.com/FOBBVCAM

Support us on our website:
https://friendsofbigbearvalley.org/

Visit our official Facebook page for posts and news from FOBBV:
https://www.facebook.com/FOBBV/

Follow our LIVE Recap & Observations for information about events-of-the-day:

https://docs.google.com/document/d/1gx7VP85Gwp1jhHRilStcZMrnUPszHQ0-w1czkjnf9bc

I watch daily on the Big Bear Bald Eagles' Jackie and Shadow Official Group. It tells so much about bald eagles and their lives as well as shows updating photos. Debra Shores is the admin.

Jackie And Shadow

I'm going to give you a bit of a breakdown of google searches of these two beautiful eagles.

Jackie and Shadow are a pair of bald eagles that live near Big Bear Lake in California and have captivated audiences with their lives.

Discovery

Jackie first came to the public's attention in 2017 when she and Shadow took over an abandoned nest with cameras installed nearby. Shadow joined the nest the following year.

Live streaming

The friends of Big Bear Valley group live-stream gained significant attention in 2023 when Jackie and Shadow tried to hatch eggs despite heavy snow.

As of February 2024, Jackie and Shadow have laid over fourteen eggs, five of which have hatched. They have had three chicks survive to fledgling.

Dynamics

Jackie and Shadow are a model of cooperation, taking turns incubating eggs and hunting for food. They have a strong bond, but they also have playful disagreements, like gentle beak nudges or playful nips.

Habitat

Jackie and Shadow live in a crucial habitat area on an undeveloped parcel of land on the north shore of Big Bear Lake.

Internet Fame

Jackie and Shadow have become internet-famous, and fans around the world are deeply attached to them. Jackie, believed to be the first eaglet hatched in Big Bear Valley, came to the public's attention in 2017 when she and her mate took over an abandoned nest with two cameras

Soaring Along with God's Love

installed beside it, while Shadow came to the public's attention one year later, when he replaced Jackie's mate at the nest.

Pure Joy

Jackie is the female eagle and Shadow is the male. They are so beautiful and magnificent to look at. You can tell the difference of them by Jackie's beak for one: It is larger, thicker, and longer than Shadow's. Her body size is also larger than his. They have been together for years.

As you watch Jackie and Shadow on YouTube and Facebook, you will see the love they have for one another. He takes good care of her and in each of their behaviors. They both show love and sadness, but then they go on about their lives. It reminds me in the Bible as some would mourn and tear their clothing during these times.

Shadow loved her so much he ran off Mr. B (her first mate) so he could be with her. Eagles usually mate for life, but these two are one different situation. They have to show their independence and strong ability to survive and do life their way. That's what makes them so fantastic and amazing to watch. I am so addicted to their every move. It's just fascinating and majestic.

Jackie and Shadow

Nest Renovations

As I watch Jackie and Shadow build on to their nest renovating for the next family they attempt to hatch and raise, they arrange their sticks perfectly, and sometimes they disagree how one should be placed. It is the cutest thing to see them pull and tug on a stick deciding the exact place in the nest for that particular one. Eventually they agree to disagree, and it is put in its perfect spot. Of course, I have seen them move them around several different time during nest building. They take turns flying with sticks, and then before long, they bring in fluff (that is little piles of soft tissue, like grass). That is just old grass to make it softer for the eggs to lie on.

Dinner Time

They will bring each other fish for dinner. It's amazing to see Jackie use her vocals to a loud screech when she sees Shadow coming with her fish. She screams and screeches so loud I'm sure the whole forest knows what is happening. I often wonder what eagle language is by all that screeching. It brings a smile to my face to see they are so human-like.

Soaring Along with God's Love

Fiona And Fast Freddie

FOBBV group posted this 10/31/2024. *THE CHORTLER PRESENTS: FIONA*

"And now! Straight from the Eagles Nest of Jackie and Shadow, we present *FIONA*! From humble beginnings, this furry rodent, also known as a (SBFS) San Bernardino Flying Squirrel, rose to global fame on this stage of sticks.

Performing nocturnally, Fiona can be seen and heard chattering, chomping, and cavorting. Fiona continues to excite nest watchers as she zooms around the habitat, eats a beetle, and plays tag with Fast Freddie, another *SBFS*. Their antics have served to present knowledge about this special breed. Fiona and Fast Freddie reside in a secluded nest that is not available for public view. Hence, the Lodge pole Chipmunk emoji for privacy purposes. Stay tuned for the nightly escapades of our Famous Fiona."

Jackie And Shadows History Of Chicks

In 2018, Jackie and Shadow laid two eggs in the same nest, *BBB* and Stormy. *BBB* died, but Stormy was seen around the lake on its own.

In 2019, Simba hatched and fledged in July. He left Big Bear Valley and was last seen at the nest on August

Jackie and Shadow

18, 2019. Cookie hatched also in 2019 and died of hypothermia during a snowstorm and freezing rain on Memorial Day weekend.

In 2020 and 2021, Jackie's clutches of eggs were either eaten by ravens or didn't hatch.

In 2022, Jackie and Shadow's eaglet, Spirit, was born and was considered a miracle baby by many.

Jackie has lost about a dozen eggs and eaglets in more than ten years in Big Bear Valley. She has braved blizzards and fought off countless enemies

Isaiah 40:31 says, "But they that wait upon the Lord shall renew their strength."

Nesting Time For Jackie And Shadow

Jackie and Shadow will turn their eggs as needed and watch closely over them.

Deuteronomy 32:11 (NIV): "Like an eagle stirs up its nest and hovers over its young, that spreads its wings to catch them and carries them on it pinions."

Rarely do they both leave the nest because predators will attack the eggs. One year, the ravens did it, and it was heartbreaking when they came back to the nest. They roll those eggs on a schedule to keep them viable. (Sometimes they may not hatch anything; that is when it's so emotional to see.)

Soaring Along with God's Love

When an eaglet or two hatch, it is amazing to watch how they are such a huge bird to be so careful to feed their eaglets, taking off tiny pieces of a fish or what they are feeding and touching the beak of the little one. They rarely lay three eggs that hatch, but sometimes, when they do, the youngest doesn't make it. The others are larger than it, and if hungry, they will devour the little one. It is a sight I would rather not see.

Some years, it is just a sad thing to watch when they try so hard. It gives me hope to see that even an eagle is strong and doesn't give up. Jackie sits on that nest no matter what the weather, and she will not allow Shadow to help her in the snow or bad weather. She sits there for days until the winter storm is over. They are dedicated more than some humans are. It's so sad to watch how hard they work when nature just doesn't produce the eaglets they try so hard to hatch. You can see the stress in their eyes when time had gone too long. It's hard to take in that such a strong beautiful creature struggles with infertility just like some of us humans do.

There are comments posted from fans across the world, amazed at their beauty and sad when they are sad.

These two will roost in a tree near the nest. They have a front porch branch they sit on and will fly off. It's a sight to see these two come into the nest and land in the center of it. Even with eggs in the nest bowl, they land carefully to not harm them. *FOBBV* always show videos and stories that entice and excite my heart to the fullest.

October 22, 2024, *BBBE FB* page posted this information I thought was wonderful.

While it is true that eagles build on their nest all the time, during fall, their primary focus is preparing the nest specifically for egg laying, incubation, and raising their chick(s). The big sticks being brought in provide a dual purpose. They serve as a barrier (guardrails for the crib, so to speak), keeping the chicks safely in the nest bowl until they are old enough to begin the practice of perching and branching. Smaller branches are used for shaping and fortifying the nest and nest bowl. Often, larger sticks are broken down to be placed "just right," as we all know how particular our Shadow can be.

But inquiring minds want to know…*WHERE'S DA FLUFF*?!

So, let's talk *FLUFF*…What exactly is fluff? These are the soft materials that the Eagles bring in to line the nest bowl (or center of the nest), to create a soft, warm nursery just right for eggs and chicks. Each territory provides a different type of available fluff. For Jackie and Shadow, it typically consists of pine needles, grasses, and reeds from the shoreline. Normally, we will not see

Soaring Along with God's Love

signs of "fluff" until Jackie is ready to start the egg-laying process, with more delivered often after eggs are laid. However, she did grace us with the 1st fluff of the season on 10/14/24 this year. Jackie always keeps us on our toes. BBBE page shows us pictures of the fluff. Fluff is not always necessary for success—just nice to have!

All this is to say, cast your worries aside! Jackie and Shadow are pros at nest building and will do what is needed to make their nest effect, and we are honored to be here watching this step-by-step process.

Stay tuned as we follow Jackie and Shadow through this season's activities! Enjoy the nest, every birdie, and happy watching. Much gratitude to *FOBBV* for the knowledge and enjoyment provided. Thanks to Cali Condor for the awesome screen captures!

This post was from the Facebook page I mentioned above. It's absolutely a real live drama of happiness and tears as you watch the lives of these two eagles. Last year was a hard one, but they survived and are back at it with grace and joy.

I am going to include another post from 10/21/24 from their Facebook page. I want you to see just the excitement the volunteers provide for us watchers.

"Happy Monday, Oct 212024 everyone!

You just never know!! Not to be outdone by Shadow

Jackie and Shadow

bringing a stick to the nest Sunday evening, Jackie flies in with a Pine cone! Our wonderful *FOBBV* cam operators gave us a great zoom of Jackie's pride and Joy! Beside their evening visit to the nest, Jackie and Shadow were in the Roost tree and on the Look out Snag Sunday morning, and in the Stick Depot Snag and Twin Pine. They are making good use of their various sentry trees in the habitat.

We had visits at the nest from Steller's Jay, White-breasted Nuthatch, Western Bluebirds, Red-breasted Sapsucker, Pygmy Nuthatch, Red-Breasted Sapsucker, Pygmy Nuthatch, Red-Breasted Nuthatch and Mountain Chickadee. A Band-tailed Pigeon stopped by the Cactus Snag."

The above is an example of what each day is like watching the lives of Jackie and Shadow. I can't wait to log on each day to see their new shenanigans they participate in with each other. It's pure joy and is good to keep your mind on positive and happy thoughts. I am so thankful I was introduced to these lovely eagles. I hope that you will take one time to go to the FOBBV page and see what happens; I really think it will bring you joy also. Just keep in mind, the joy we have in life is brought to us by our Lord and Savior.

Last season was a very intense season with Jackie and

Shadow, waiting on her first egg to be laid, then second, and she laid a third (which is unusual, I believe). Jackie and Shadow fought the bad weather, wind, storms, heat, and cold. They are troopers and did it without a hitch. In and out of the nest, it was the most amazing thing to see those huge wings come in so gracefully. Sometimes a fuss over a stick and then a beaky kiss.

Watching them sit in the lookout snag tree together of the mornings and chortle together, I always wonder what they must be saying to one another. I love to see them throw their heads back and call out to the other one.

https://www.allaboutbitds.org/guide/Steller_Jay

https://www.allaboutbirds.org/guide/White-breasted_nuthatch

https:/.www.allaboutbirds.org/guide/Western_bluebird

https://www.allaboutbirds.org,/guide/mountain_

Chickadee

https://www.allaboutbirds.org/guide/Band-tailed_
Pigeon.

These links will show you a bit about the birds that visit.

Enjoy!

My Whole Excitement From The Eagles

My heart changing and the eagle watching all started about the same time. I realized there was more than what I had been taught or seen in worshiping Jesus. I wasn't satisfied with just existing as a Christian. It's like the eagles; I was never satisfied with seeing one and never going eagle watching again. The more we see of Jesus, the more we should want. I do not want to hear Him say I was lukewarm, that he never knew me. I will even go for a drive alone just to see what I can find to watch on any given day. That is the best thing about fall and winter: The leaves have fallen, and the eagles are easier to spot in the trees. It makes a better photograph with no leaves to interfere with the focus of the camera.

I love to watch an eagle sitting on the nest and another one on a lookout branch. It's so beautiful to know they have each other's back. They take turns sitting and

Soaring Along with God's Love

hunting for each other, and it's just spectacular.

I get so blessed by just watching Jackie and Shadow on YouTube or their Facebook page, live videos of them flying in the nest and sitting on their front porch, the pinecone Jackie loves to decorate with. She will rearrange it, and it slides right back where it was to begin with. She is so persistent. I have often wandered if she wanted to pitch it out of the nest, but not Jackie; she loves that pinecone.

When Jackie and Shadow sit in front of that camera like no one is watching, it's just a miracle to me. They are just so beautiful; I can't get enough of them. It's the same way I feel when I learn something new in the Bible when that story never made sense before or the Holy Spirit reveals something to my heart.

As they turn those eggs so gently and wiggle down slowly to sit on the eggs, it's amazing; they are so smart and know what to do. I could sit for hours and watch them and make up little stories that fit right in with how they are acting. I thank God each time I see an eagle in the wild. Every so often, one will fly over my car and make circles. I think to myself, they are showing off their beauty and they know how much I enjoy it.

Jackie and Shadow

Jackie and Shadow are so devoted to their eggs throughout the incubation process. There are times that winter storms pass through and Jackie will not leave the nest. She sat for days last year, trying her best to protect her babies from the elements. The eggs didn't turn out to be viable, but not because of her lack of knowledge or effort. She is such a beauty; most people watching daily can't get enough of them. Every single day, I see love in so many ways between those two.

CHAPTER NINE

Why do I See the Holy Spirit

As you have seen some photos of Shadow and Jackie and scriptures that can be balanced by what I have witnessed, I hope that you can see why I have gravitated to the eagle family.

Sometimes we as humans can't see danger in beauty; we need to stay prayed up and focus on what the Word tells us and the Holy Spirit relays to us.

John 14:26-27 (NIV): "But the counselor the Holy Spirit, whom the Father will send in my name, will teach you all things and will remind you of everything I have said to you. Peace I leave with you; my peace I give you."

The Father wanted us to keep the teachings of Jesus' life and share with others. Letting it die as a lot of this world is doing is not a plan of God's. He taught us to love our neighbor and to keep peace to the best of our ability. I sure wish that all the plans Jesus had for me from day one I would have followed as tightly as possible to keep. When we do not follow His Word or rebel against His scriptures in teaching us, it always brings us pain. That has happened to me in life so many times. God loves us unconditionally and wants us to remember that most

Soaring Along with God's Love

of all. We have to pick ourselves back up and ask for wisdom and knowledge to not do the same things again. God shows me how He would rather I handle a situation like this next time, with love and understanding the best I can. Most of our own pain we have can be brought on by our own choices.

We can be standing at a crossroad knowing the choice we want to make, or the words we choose to say are not what God would approve. We still choose to do the wrong choice. As my aunt would say to me when I am upset at myself, "Well, how did that work out for you?" After a few times of messing up something without thinking what I should do, I have to ask myself that. Chances are, I did not ask God before making that move, or it would have turned out different. Then there I go having to apologize and/or live with grief I brought on myself.

God knows we aren't perfect, but how many times do people say they wished life, parenting, and other things came with a handbook? We are equipped with one; we just have to read it and do the best we can to learn from it. People judge each other by one act they saw that was negative from someone and do not pay attention to what good they did, trying to be obedient. Remember, folks: try to spare the stone we throw because we have our own issues. Not one of us can change the past, but we must do

Why do I See the Holy Spirit

our best to change the present. We do not live in our past anymore. Jesus took our sins, and they are non-existent.

CHAPTER TEN

Prison Fellowship

My Journey

One day after I got off at work, I had that mom gut feeling that something was wrong. I made a phone call, asking if anyone had seen my son. No, they hadn't, but he was okay last time they did. That very next morning at 1:00am, my phone rang. It was his girlfriend telling me he had been arrested. I called the police station and spoke to an officer. They were processing him at the time. They said he was lucky he was okay and not hurt or worse. The officer even allowed me to speak to him. I don't even remember the conversation; I was so upset.

The next day I went to see him. I visited every time I was allowed when he was close by. The first time, I believe he was nineteen years old. I remember the tears flowing when I saw him through that glass window and having to speak through a phone. My heart broke, and I just couldn't handle the stress. I cried so much, knowing things were so different than I had hoped for him.

The day he had to go to court, I was waiting for him at the back steps of the courthouse where the inmates

Soaring Along with God's Love

would come through. My husband and I was standing there, and as my eyes caught him walking across, my knees went weak. He was in shackles and chains! I started shaking and crying and was beside myself. My handsome son was in an orange suite, chained, and now with a criminal record.

As we went inside to the courtroom, I saw officers sitting to my right, the judge straight in front of me. My knees were shaking and my heart pounding so hard. One of the officers came to me and knelt down and asked if I was his mother. I said yes. He began to tell me he was going to be okay; he was the arresting officer. When he pulled my son out of the truck after crashing at over 100mph, the first thing my son said was, "I need help," He said, "I have never heard someone say that, and I think he learned his lesson." Rightfully. It could have been so much worse. I knew he was into things that were not right. He used to call me late at night and tell me things that scared me for his life. I just prayed God would keep him safe. I believe that was around 2001, and I had never heard much of overdoses like today. I was so worried about him being so high he would hurt himself or others.

He was ordered rehab and went there for three weeks shy of three months. He looked so happy and so good.

Prison Fellowship

He had gained weight, and I knew in my heart it was all going to be okay now.

Shortly after that, there was round two: He was arrested again. This time, he got six months in prison. I drove to see him as often as I could; he was a couple hours away, and I had a full-time job. We talked often, and that was when we still had a home phone and he could call collect. I allowed him to call anytime he wanted. My phone bill was little over $300 a month. I didn't care; I wanted to help him however it was or whatever it took. I sent him money occasionally for the commissary so he could get decent food and a television. I got letters from him, and I still have them; I sent a lot of pictures of my beagle. Finally, one day he said, "Mom, I have a hundred pictures of that dog; I don't think I need anymore."

When it came time for him to get out, we had big plans. I was going to get him an apartment, clothes, and furniture donated by family to get him started. He was so excited, and so was I. Not long after that, I went back to see him (he lived an hour and half from me, in our hometown); he was lying on the couch, high again. I was just sick to my stomach and knew this wasn't going to last long at this pace.

A year or so later, there he was again, back in jail.

Soaring Along with God's Love

This time, he was sentenced five years; he served half of that. He was further away from me that time, so the visits were not as often. I refused to send money—only for Christmas and his birthday, and it wasn't much. I wanted him to feel the pain of being there and not having everything he wanted to make it easier.

When time came to get him, I was so excited because he was transferred the last year to a place he could work and get less time. He did great at it, so I thought he had learned his lesson. I picked him up, got his clothes, apartment, and groceries. It was not long until he was back at doing the same thing again. He had asked me to take him to another rehab near me. I took him, dropped him off, and by the end of the day, he had hitched a ride to my house. I would not allow him to stay there because he would not follow rules and get straight.

He had gotten his *GED* while in rehab or prison, and when my daughter graduated with her associates degree, we had a double celebration. He was clean at the time and so proud that it looked like things were getting better.

He asked if he could stay here with us. My husband and I said only if he found a job and only a few days. I took him the next day to job hunt. He got one right off the bat, and I was so proud. He worked hard and did really well. He eventually found an apartment, and he moved

Prison Fellowship

there. He had no driver's license, so I got up at 4:00am on weekends, and then he had to be at work at 6:00am on weekdays. I didn't have to be at work till 8:00am, so I had to kill so much time. Every morning, he would hate me to talk to him and was rude and not thankful.

A year later, my husband and I had helped him get to places so he could get his license back. Then we helped him get a truck, and he paid us back. I was so happy he was back to normal, and I was enjoying him. We did things together, and I would go visit him and help him with his apartment.

Then he met a woman with three kids living with her. He fell in love and wanted to move into our extra double wide we had. He was starting to have an attitude again, and I felt something was wrong. He and the woman were together about three years.

One day, she told us he was using again and what was going on. She had been a mess herself, so I wasn't so sure it was all true. I did know something just wasn't right. They split up, and he continued to go downhill. He trashed the double wide, and we had to force him to move. We tore down the double wide; we weren't having anything to do with this again. He would go from rehab to homeless and back to rehabs but never stay with anything. He didn't like rules and would rebel at

Soaring Along with God's Love

everything he did. He blamed us for losing his home. He never took the blame for his own actions.

At this time, he has been clean a couple months and is basically homeless, staying with a friend and working. I am not sure what tomorrow holds, but I know that I have to separate myself from the stress and drama before it kills me.

My Dream

The time my son was in prison, I started teaching Sunday school to pre-teenagers. I wanted to get it in their head to not use drugs or hang with the wrong crowds. I ended up teaching for eight years. I wanted to go to jails and prisons and speak with the inmates about what this does to a mother and was hopeful it would change their outcome. After what I experienced going into a prison to visit my son, my husband would not agree to it.

Not long ago, I heard of someone in jail whose mom I knew; I left church one Sunday and went to the jail. The mother and grandmother were there, broken-hearted just like I was or even worse. I asked if I could take five minutes and speak to him. They both agreed it was fine, and all three of us went in to see him. He also was behind glass, and we had to speak through a phone.

When I spoke with him, I asked him if he was sorry

Prison Fellowship

for his actions. With tears streaming down his face, he answered yes. I witnessed to him about Jesus loving him and that no matter what he had done, if he repented and asked Jesus into his heart, he was saved. It may not take the consequences away but he would have Jesus by his side through everything. I asked if he would like for me to pray with him so he could be saved. Yes, he said. We prayed and cried and rejoiced for his decision.

I knew then I still wanted to do prison fellowship. When I was telling my publisher my book wasn't going to be a big one, just to the point, he said that a lot of times books like this will go to prisons. My heart about jumped through my chest. Seriously, maybe this is exactly the prison fellowship God has put before me to go along with visits. I'm not giving up on the personal visits to one, and I plan to proceed and find out what I need to do. If it could change one person's heart in prison and help them see the pain it causes others…it would all be worth it.

CHAPTER ELEVEN

Scriptures to Build On

Self Worth

James 4:10 (NIV): "Humble yourselves before the Lord, and He will lift you up."

Ephesians 1:17-19 (NIV): "I keep asking that the God of our Lord Jesus Christ, the glorious Father, may give you the Spirit of wisdom and revelation, so that you may know him better. I pray that the eyes of your heart may be enlightened in order that you may know the hope to which he has called you, the riches of his glorious inheritance in his holy people, and his incomparably great power for us who believe. That power is like the working of mighty strength."

Jeremiah 9:23-24 (NIV): "This is what the LORD says: 'Let not the wise boast of their wisdom or the strong boast of their strength or the rich boast of their riches, but let the one who boasts boast about this: that they have the understanding to know me, that I am the LORD, who exercises kindness, justice and righteousness on earth, for in these I delight,' declares the LORD."

Romans 8:28-29 (NIV): "And we know that in all

Soaring Along with God's Love

things God works for good of those who love him, who have been called according to his purpose. For those God fore-knew he also predestined to be conformed to the likeness of his Son, that he might be the firstborn among many brothers."

Anxiety/Worry

Proverbs 12:25 (NIV): "…an anxious heart weighs a man down, but a kind word cheers it up."

1 Peter 5:7 (NIV): "Cast all your anxiety on him because he cares for you."

Philippians 4:6-7 (NIV): "Do not be anxious about anything, but in everything by prayer and petition, with thanksgiving, present your request to God. And the peace of God, which transcends all understanding, will guard your hearts and your mind in Christ Jesus."

SOME TEACHING MOMENTS

For the most part, the eagle stories that have been told I think will really encourage you. At this time, I want to share a few things with you that I have seen on social media and other places that just inspire me. I do hope that you will take the time to continue with reading and feel what I have. This is a huge game changer in Christianity and not religion. I'm to the point I do not even like to hear the word religion, because I don't feel that is what it is. To my heart, it is a relationship with Jesus. I'm so far

Scriptures to Build On

from perfect and fail daily, but you know that God loves all of us and wants the best for us. That is why I thrive on reading posts, scriptures, and commentaries, even if they do convict me (step on my toes, so to speak). I will never be what I want to be, but I will hopefully be better than I was yesterday and today. As you read my feelings from my heart in this book, I hope you pray for God to touch your heart and open your mind to his wisdom. I love the posts by Barry Bennett; he feeds me what I need to hear. I hope the same for you. This is pretty much what I was just saying about religion.

Our lives and our health are under our authority. Religion has taught us that God is responsible for our lives and whether we have health, victory, or prosperity. But fatalistic religion is wrong. God has given His people His authority. We will either enforce His will, or we will become passive and allow the enemy to steal, kill, and destroy.

Ephesians 3:20 (NIV): "Now to Him who is able to do immeasurably more than all we ask or imagine, according to his power that is at work within us."

Proverbs 18:21 (NIV): "The tongue has the power of life and death, and those who love it will eat its fruit."

Soaring Along with God's Love

Entering into the Victory!

By Barry Bennett

"So many try and understand Christianity from a place of minimal knowledge mixed with their feelings and emotions. This approach usually brings frustration and even hopelessness. There are foundational truths that need to be understood for the Word of God to come alive to you and activate your faith.

Do you understand the difference between the law of sin and death, and the law of the Spirit of life in Christ Jesus? We must understand the tremendous difference between the results of Adam's sin, and the results of the finished work of Christ on our behalf.

If you are born again, do you understand the Old Covenant and the New? So many make no distinction between the two covenants and get confused when trying to understand the true gospel.

Do you understand the power of darkness vs. the Kingdom of God? We must realize that we have been transferred from the power of darkness into the Kingdom of God if we are going to begin to learn how to live in His Kingdom.

Do you know that when you were born again, you

Scriptures to Build On

were made new and that God/Christ/the Holy Spirit came to reside in you? You are a new creation. You are no longer limited to your own thoughts, emotions, and will power. You have God's Spirit within!

Do you understand righteousness by faith? Do you know that Christ bore our sin and curse on the cross and that He has gifted us His righteousness? Jesus sat down at the right hand of God because God was satisfied with His victory over sin, Satan, and death. We have now received the gift of His righteousness!

Do you understand the nature of Satan and the nature of God? We must know that God is not the 'thief' that comes to steal, kill, and destroy! God is for you, wants to bless you, and give you the kingdom!

These truths need to be understood in our hearts for the life of faith and victory to be real.

'My people are destroyed for lack of knowledge' (Hosea 4:6).

Those who are free in the Lord don't talk like those who are in bondage. Those who are in bondage speak of their fears, their symptoms, their anxieties, and their needs. Those who are free use the gift of words to speak of Jesus' victory, guilt-free living, love, joy, peace, faith, healing, and blessings.

'Therefore if the Son makes you free, you shall be

Soaring Along with God's Love

free indeed' (John 8:36).

'Stand fast therefore in the liberty by which Christ has made us free, and do not be entangled again with a yoke of bondage' (Galatians 5:1).

'Death and life are in the power of the tongue, and those who love it will eat its fruit' (Proverbs 18:21).

God hates everything that causes poverty, sin, injustice, ignorance, laziness, and sickness. God's prosperity begins at the new birth and continues with the renewing of the mind, the fruit of the Spirit, His love to give and forgive, healing, and the fruits of righteousness. Jesus called it abundant life!"

Final Closing Thoughts

I have learned so much and wish I could undo a lot in my life, although that's not possible. God wants us to move forward and put the past behind us. If we don't change the way we do things, we will not get a better outcome. I have had to learn a lot of hard lessons in life, but learning is what it's all about. Hurt others and being hurt is a hard landing. Forgiveness is a must; forgive those that don't even ask for it. Be sure to forgive yourself as well; beating yourself up does not solve anything. Holding grudges doesn't pay back a person; it only makes a person bitter and form a hard heart. Life sure makes that hard to do a lot of times. The Word of God tells us in Ephesians 4:31-32 (NIV), "Get rid of all bitterness, rage and anger, brawling and slander, along with every form of malice. Be kind and compassionate to one another, forgiving each other, just as Christ God forgave you."

Matthew 6:14-15 (NIV): "For if you forgive other people when they have sinned against you, your heavenly Father will also forgive you. But if you do not forgive other men their sins, your Father will not forgive your sins."

Sins cannot be removed but can be forgiven. You are

Soaring Along with God's Love

releasing yourself when forgiving. That's very hard to do when your motives have been taken out of content or you asked for forgiveness and it was refused. I think the hardest for me is when the pain is so deep and the person never acknowledges your request for forgiveness; and the other heartbreak is when they don't see any wrong-doing in their actions. Give it to the Lord to sort out; it will be a lot less stressful and painful.

There is so much hatred in our world now—it is absolutely scary. Everyone is out to get the other person regardless of what it does to their reputation or heart. I have been on both sides in my life, and it's never a good thing to suffer. We must be brave to treat each other with respect; it is just so hard to undo when that fine line is crossed. So many times, hurting people hurt others. You never know what is hurting them so bad inside; it's always good to have empathy. Ask God for strength to get past it and move on with life.

Sometimes setting some healthy boundaries is never a bad thing. I have learned a few things in my own life. There are several principles that we can learn from eagles; I am sure there are more that could be put in good use.

Stay away from narrow-minded people, those that bring you down or belittle you. Forgiveness is granted at

Final Closing Thoughts

the same time trust is earned. I say that meaning we must forgive always, but we can distance ourselves for mental health reasons. I used to believe I had to take anything dished out to me, and then I would blow up. I now know that is not a healthy way to practice being a child of God. Have a vision and remain focused no matter what the obstacles, and you will succeed.

Do not rely on your past success; keep looking for new goals to conquer. Leave your past where it belongs: in the past. Eagles run off invaders and do not allow those that could danger their home, eaglets, or mates. We should guard our hearts the same.

Face your challenges ahead knowing that these will make you emerge stronger and better than you were. We can use the storms of life to rise to greater heights. Eagles sometimes fly to great heights to avoid a storm. Achievers are not afraid to rise to greater heights, challenges; rather, they relish them and use them profitably.

I enjoy so much of the eagle stories I have told in this book. I hope you have felt my excitement through the book. I truly felt the Holy Spirit told me I should share that how magnificent I think the eagles are is how He feels about us. We see the eagles, but we can't see Him; for those of us that have a relationship with Him instead of religion, it's a whole new view. We study His

Soaring Along with God's Love

Word, and it's so powerful, just like the eagles' wings are. Their talons and beaks are so strong and dangerous but so beautiful. Just like the Holy Spirit, they both require respect in my opinion.

I do know while writing this book it has even shown me things in my life that I need to improve. It also excites me to think I may help someone else struggling with big or small things in life. Give it to Jesus and let him help you.

I must add at this point I do hope that you are a child of God saved by grace, that you believe that he died on the cross, rose again, and was ascended to Heaven. He sent the Holy Spirit to lead, guide, and direct us. I pray that for each and every one of you reading this book that if you have not done so that you will now. Ask Jesus into your heart!

A prayer that I love to know others have said for salvation:

"Lord Jesus, I come to you asking that you forgive me of my sins and come into my heart. I want to be a born-again Christian and live for you every day of my life. Thank you, Lord, for this opportunity, and I welcome the Holy Spirit in my life to lead, guide, and direct me the way you would intend. Keep me humble and loving as you desire. Amen!"

Final Closing Thoughts

If you have said this prayer, I wish you would contact a Christian and follow through with baptism. It doesn't matter what you have done in your life; nothing is too much for Jesus. His arms are open to you, and He wants you in Heaven with Him some day. I would encourage you to start reading in the New Testament and learn all about Jesus and what He has done. He has so much in store for you. Life will always have trials and tribulations for Christians and non-Christians. Now that you have made that decision, you will not go through anything alone. He is by your side 24/7 and will hear every word your heart cries.

This world is going crazy: rights are made wrong and vice versa. Do not let pride or a haughty spirit take your eternity. I would walk alone rather than be in a crowd of the wrong people. If you need to change friends and distance from those that temp or drag you down, then do so. Do not allow one person to work with Satan to steal, kill, or destroy you.

I have included several scriptures with titles that can help you as you begin your new life with Jesus. I also suggest you read Proverbs daily, just as my friend Danny Joe suggested to me years ago. Example: January 1, read Proverbs 1, and so on. It will take you a month to get through it, but as you get into the habit of reading God's

Soaring Along with God's Love

love stories, you will want more of it. The Old Testament has so many amazing things to read as well. If it's overwhelming, stick with the New Testament until you can get comfortable. I used to hate to read until I started the Proverbs schedule and then read books that I knew were from knowledgeable authors that are filled with God's knowledge.

Notes

I asked for permission before doing this, and I want to be sure and have you all know you can see them on YouTube and Facebook. The link is http://friendsofbigbearvalley.org/

This was the response to the email I sent them.

"Hello Lottie,

Yes you may use photos of Jackie and Shadow in your book, glad to know that you have decided to move forward with it. Please credit the photos to Friends of Big Bear Valley and include our web address, friendsofbigbearvalley.org, so that your readers can find the nest camera."

They have items to purchase and interesting information. Very kind folks, they have two cameras in the tree over the nest for us to get full view of Jackie and Shadow's lives. It's so fulfilling and a learning experience to watch the eagles. Even if you don't love them yet, I am sure you will after watching the lives of these amazing creatures. As I post photos that were taken by them, I will note beneath the photo. The ones I took myself will have my name attached.

Soaring Along with God's Love

I also want to thank a few friends of mine that taught me how to use a good camera and lens to take photos of wildlife. They took me places where the eagles are to instruct me the right way to identify and photo shoot them. The two that put in the most time with me were Linda Hine and the late Steve Wunderle.

"Lottie Lindsey has my permission to use my name/ info etc.

Linda Hine"

"Lottie, it's Sharon Wunderle. Congratulation on your book; Linda told me that you were in the world of authors now. Super! She also told me that Steve taught you a lot about birding and how to take great pictures. I'm sure you're doing a fantastic job, and Steve would be proud of you. I think it would be okay if you acknowledged him for that."

I messaged Barry Bennett for permission to use his posts. This was his response:

"I'm not sure which post or posts you are referring to, but you are free to use them if they aren't changed and you give credit. Blessings! You can say: Barry Bennett, Charis Bible College, Woodland Park, CO. That would be fine. Thanks for asking."

This book is about a woman and her struggles and how she grew through them and found joy through eagle photography. It will encourage readers to put God's love above anything else and make choices by His teaching. Should that not be the case of your life, the book will help you pick back up and regain your identity, regardless how others make you feel. It's all about *God's love* and what He shows us in His Word to be strong, wise, and what He intended us to be, shining that light for others to see

Soaring Along with God's Love

and enjoy being around a positive person. Learn how to remove the guilt, shame, and hurt from your heart and see yourself as God sees you.

There are several eagle photos to go along with the stories and scriptures mentioned in this book, all to build you up and bring you out of a dark place to a joyful, loving God. God loves you as you are and wants to bless you. Seeing the blessings in this little book will bring you so much joy. If you are not an eagle person, you will soon find out how one bird can change your whole thought pattern and bring you closer to the Lord.

Notes

www.ingramcontent.com/pod-product-compliance
Lightning Source LLC
LaVergne TN
LVHW011327070225
802955LV00002B/4